Wife 101
MW00438199
Everything Your Husband Wished You Already Knew

Pneuma Life
PUBLISHING

Wife 101

Everything Your Husband Wished You Already Knew

Wife 101

Editorial Director: Tiffany Hinton

Book Cover: PAZ Design Group

Printed in the United States of America

Wife 101 ISBN 1-56229-117-3

Pneuma Life Publishing
P. O. Box 885
Lanham, Maryland 20703-0885
(301) 577-4052
http://www.pneumalife.com

Introduction

Can you remember the last time you and your husband shared a special time alone together? Perhaps you spent time in an enchanted sun-swept paradise. Maybe it was an evening walk in your neighborhood as you strolled under the purple shadows of an amazing moonlit sky. Or the last time you shared a mouthwatering dessert after a special dinner celebration . . . talking in whisper-soft tones. What do you remember most about those special captivating moments? Was it a timeless sense of total connection to your husband that you remember? This books show a you how to cultivate those rapturous moments every day.

How do you maximize your results? You should read through this book several times to memorize these valuable principles and imbed them into your mind and heart. Eventually, you will automatically or involuntarily react to your spouse with the **Wife 101** actions and attitudes. It only takes twenty minutes to read through **Wife 101** and strengthen your marriage. If your spouse doesn't already have the accompaniment book **Husband 101: Everything Your Husband Wished You Already Knew**, buy a copy for him, put it under his pillow and watch him grow in love, knowledge and insight of your needs as his wife.

DO

Tell your husband that he's your hero.

DO NOT

Ignore his efforts.

DO

Record his favorite program or sporting event when he is out of town.

DO NOT

Treat him like a project in need of a major overhaul by not accepting him the way he is.

DO

Give him a massage, particularly after a hard day.

DO NOT

Spend money frivolously or live outside your means.

DO

Be conscious of his pet peeves and avoid doing them.

D
O
N
O
T

Be unwilling to try things he enjoys such as bowling, fishing, golfing, etc.

DO

Help each other to define and write out your individual and family goals.

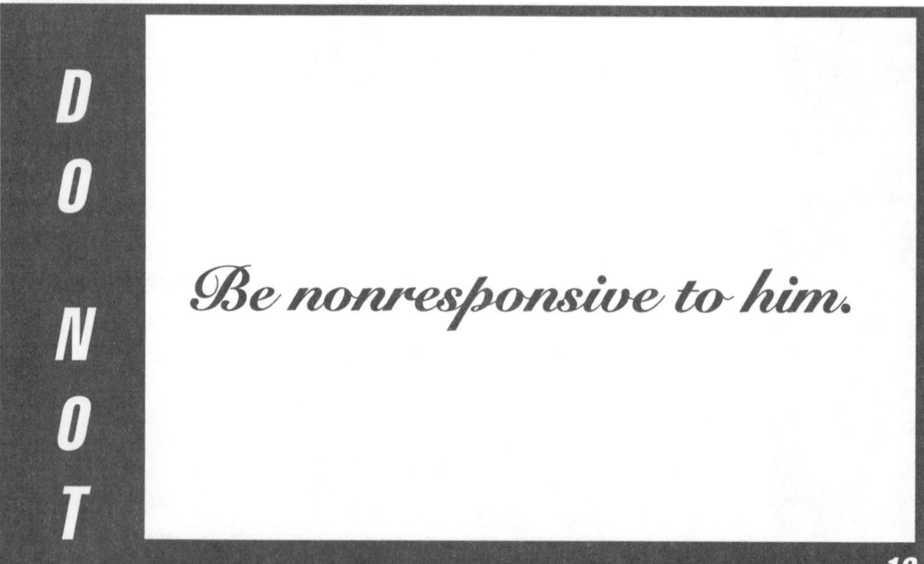
DO NOT
Be nonresponsive to him.
16

DO

Initiate sex sometimes.

D O N O T

Fail to accept responsibility for things in your relationship or always place blame on him.

DO

Tell him that he's a winner.

DO NOT

Forget to tell him that you appreciate him.

DO

Buy him books pertaining to his career and goals.

DO NOT

Destroy his hopes by continually reinforcing what he cannot do.

DO
Help to create
a family budget.
23

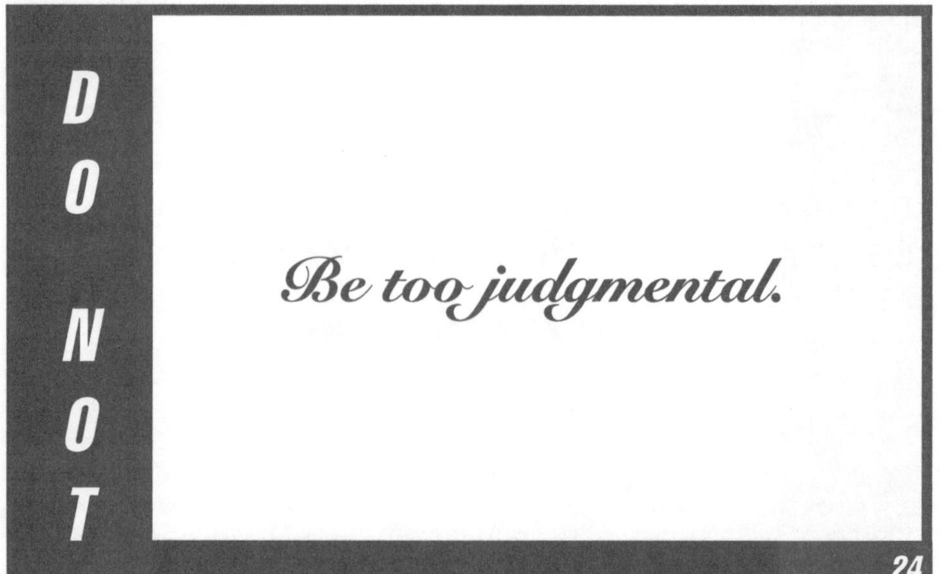
DO NOT
Be too judgmental.
24

DO

Buy and wear sexy lingerie.

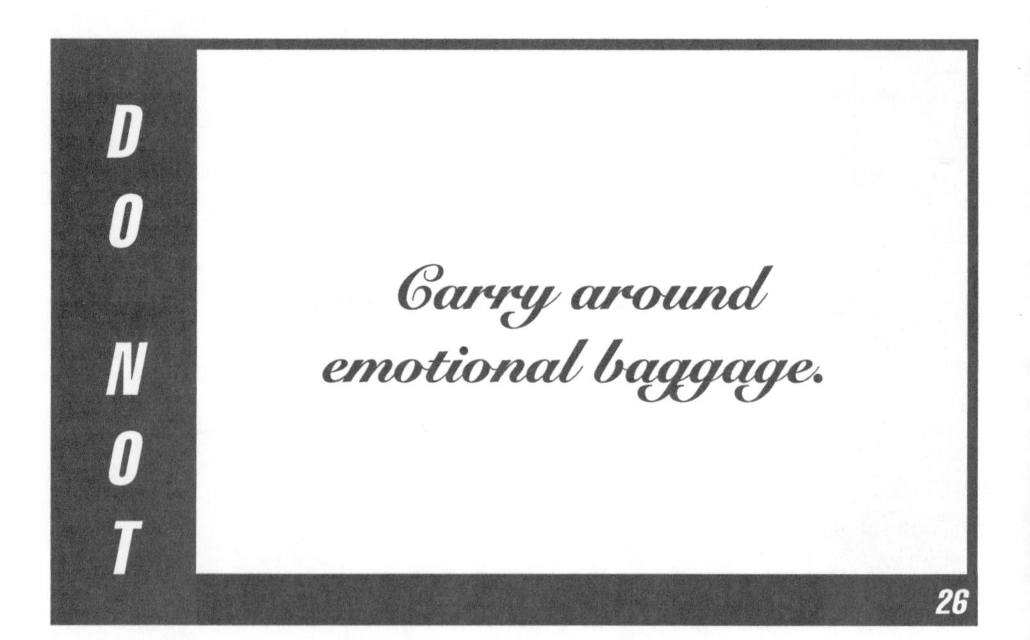
DO NOT
Carry around emotional baggage.
26

DO

Tell your husband how smart he is.

D O N O T

Exclude him when making decisions that affect the family.

DO

Let him know that you understand what he is saying when he discusses problems.

D
O
N
O
T

Make him pay for mistakes made by men from your past.

DO

Be his greatest encourager.

DO NOT

Forget to tell him just how important he is to you.

DO

Have a loving attitude.

DO NOT

Be jealous of his friends or prevent him from spending time with them.

DO

Affirm his goals, visions, and dreams.

DO NOT

Be suspicious and distrusting of him.

D
O

Tell him that you believe in him.

D O N O T

Fuss at him constantly.

DO

Be grateful and let him know that you appreciate the things he does for you and the family.

DO NOT

Be too serious, so much so that you constrict his sense of humor.

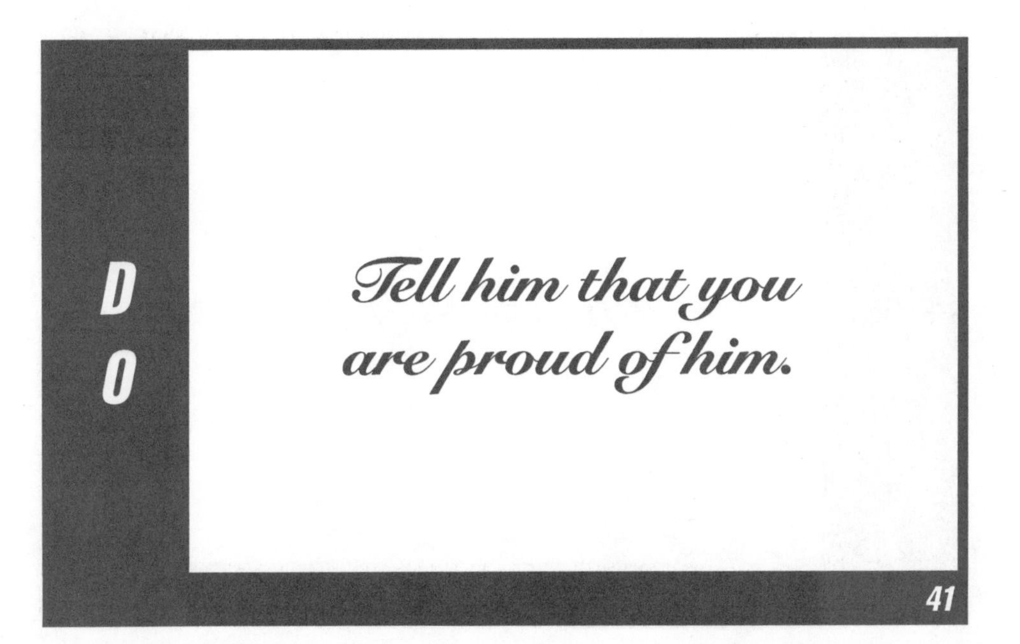
D
O
Tell him that you
are proud of him.

DO NOT
Disrespect him.
42

DO

Tell your husband about his qualities or attributes that you delight in.

D
O
N
O
T

Forget the importance of being visually appealing to him.

DO

Forego making love sometimes, and just have sex.

DO NOT

Be frigid.

DO

Save mementos from special dates—movie tickets, theater guides, airplane tickets, or hotel keys.

D
O

N
O
T

Compare him to previous boyfriends or to your father.

DO

Allow him to satisfy and please you.

DO NOT

Emasculate him through words and actions.

DO

Stimulate him visually, emotionally, intellectually, and spiritually.

DO NOT

Be paranoid.

DO

Maintain your dignity and identity.

DO NOT

Make him feel like he's not needed.

DO

Reminisce about special memories and create new ones.

D O N O T

Attack his intellect.

DO

Make a big deal out of Valentine's Day and Father's Day.

D
O
N
O
T

Embarrass him.

DO

Be direct and state your points clearly.

DO NOT

Forget to tell him that you are proud of him.

DO

Spend time relaxing, laughing, having fun, and just enjoying each other.

DO NOT

Mother him as though he's incapable of making wise decisions.

DO

Ask about his sexual needs and fulfill them.

DO NOT

Crush his spirit by killing his dreams.

DO

Be responsive and receptive to your husband.

DO NOT

Nag him.

DO

Continue to learn and grow.

DO NOT

Make him feel as though he cannot please you or make you happy.

DO

Be thoughtful and considerate of his feelings.

DO NOT

Overanalyze his every word and action.

D
O

Explore your husband mind, body, and soul.

DO NOT

Spend too much
time in organizations
which exclude him.

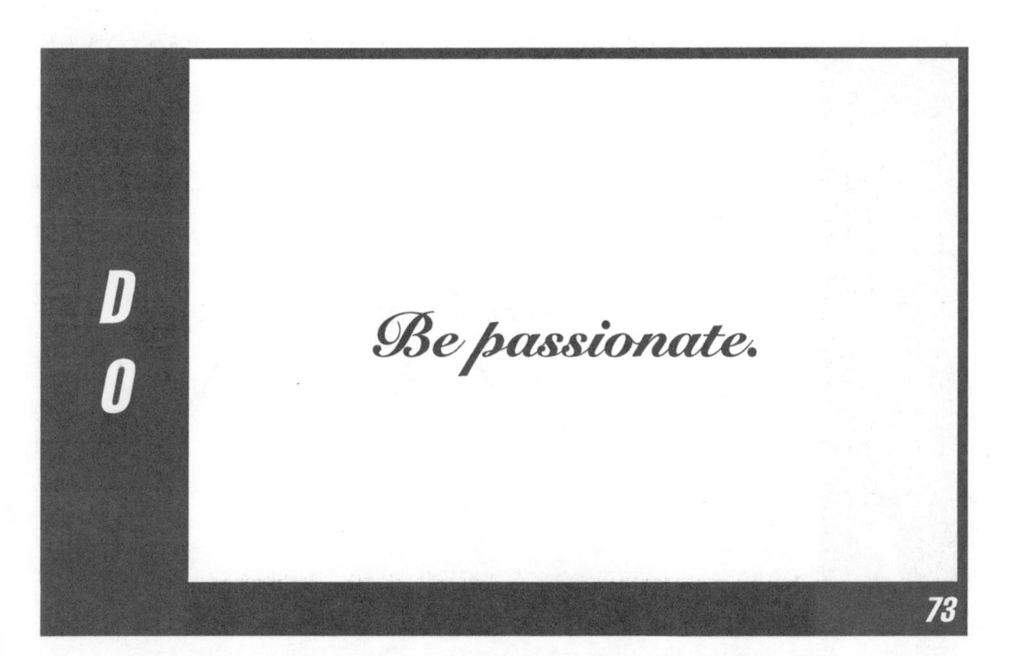
D
O
Be passionate.

DO NOT

Withhold sex as a means of punishing him.

DO

Play romantic games. For example, challenge him on who can be the most romantic in a week.

DO NOT

Make him compete for your attention.

DO

Let him buy things that are just for him and not for the family.

DO NOT

Smother him or deny him time to himself.

D
O

Love him freely.

DO NOT

Be rude to him in public.

DO

Massage his scalp, eyebrows, and temples.

D O N O T

Be irritated and annoyed with him constantly.

DO

Enhance your sensuality.

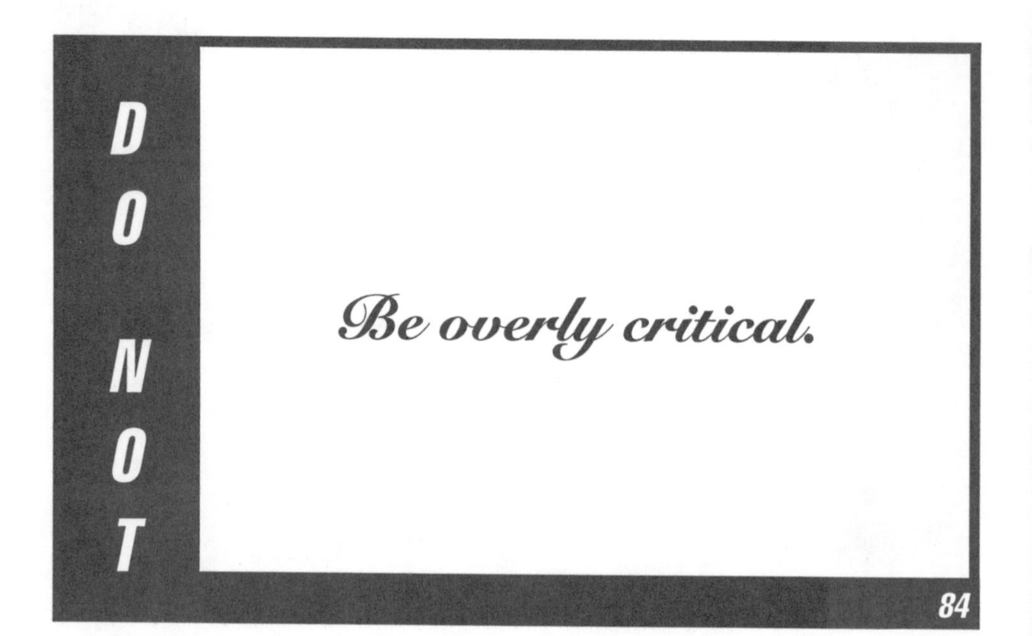
DO NOT
Be overly critical.
84

DO

Be creative, spontaneous, adventurous, and romantic.

DO NOT

Sleep separately due to disagreements and arguments.

DO

Tell him how much better your life is with him in it.

DO NOT

Bad mouth his parents or family members.

DO

Choose appropriate times in which to discuss matters of importance.

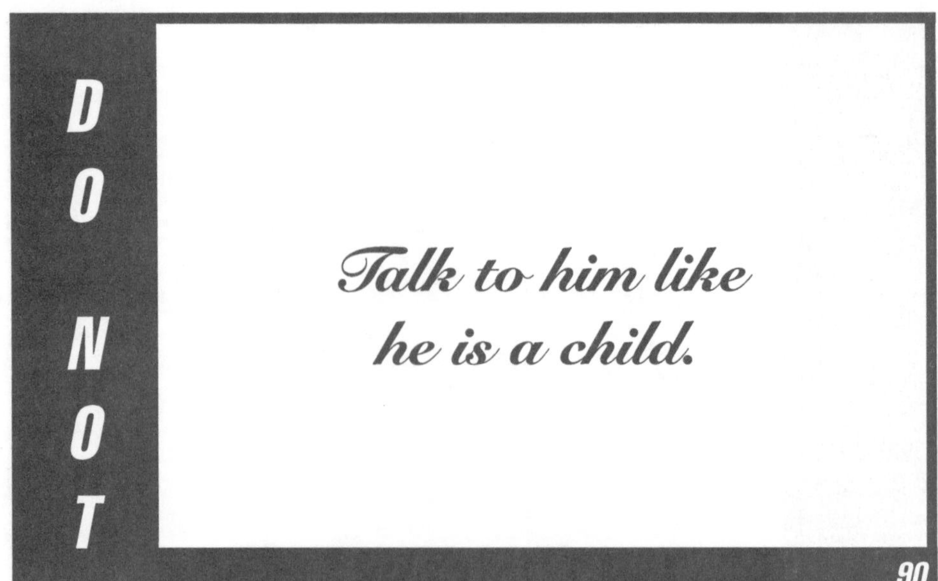

DO NOT
Talk to him like he is a child.

DO

Tell him that everything will be all right.

DO NOT

Be deceptive.

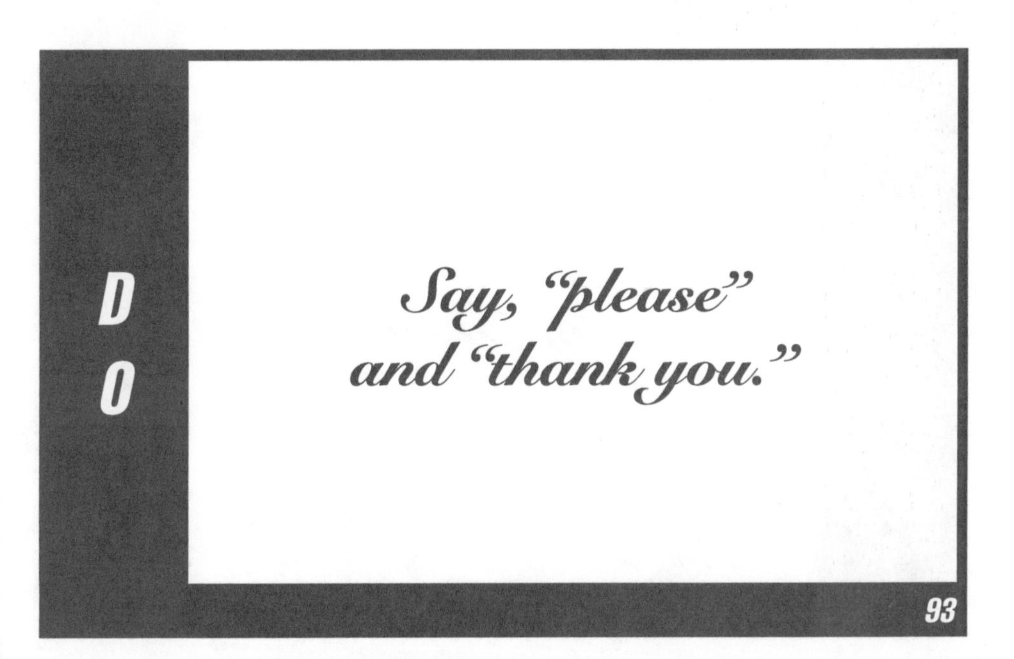
DO
Say, "please"
and "thank you."

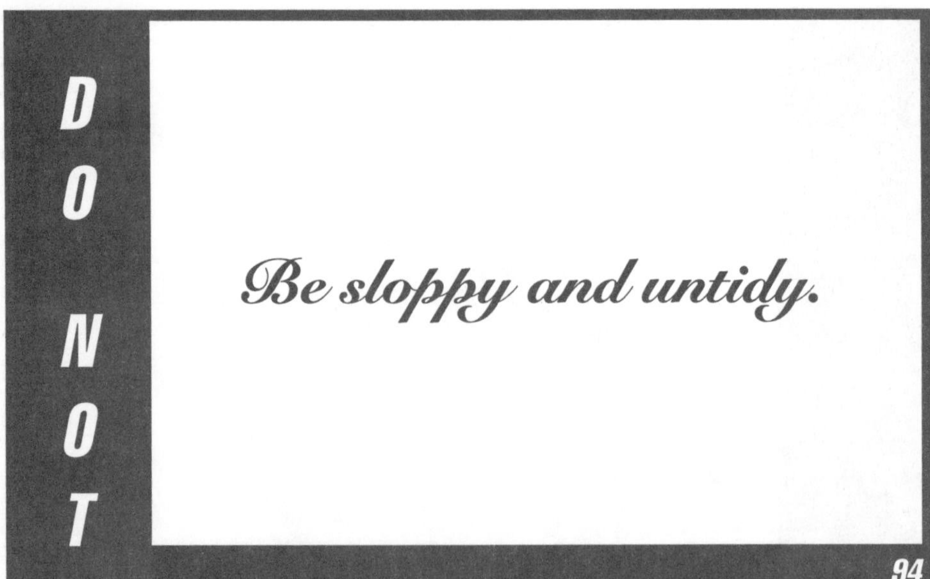
DO NOT
Be sloppy and untidy.

DO

Tell him that he can do it.

DO NOT
Condemn him.
96

DO

Offer constructive criticism.

DO NOT

Lack feminine hygiene.

DO

Tell him what you want and need. Don't assume he is a mind reader or that he already knows.

DO NOT

Always throw past mistakes in his face.

DO

Take time to ask him about his day after he's had a chance to relax.

DO NOT
Complain all of the time.
102

DO

Praise him for his achievements.

DO NOT

Insult his character and integrity.

DO

Acknowledge his efforts.

DO NOT
Belittle him.
106

DO

Let him know that you accept him.

DO NOT

Fail to recognize his accomplishments and achievements.

DO

Listen attentively to what he is saying without interrupting him.

DO NOT
Ignore him.
110

DO

Help him to visualize his goals and dreams.

DO NOT

Use guilt as a means of oppressing him.

DO

Learn how to arouse within him the desire to succeed.

DO NOT

Loud-talk him in public.

DO

Develop good health and fitness habits.

DO NOT
Reject him.
116

DO

Continue to focus on your own goals, dreams, and aspirations.

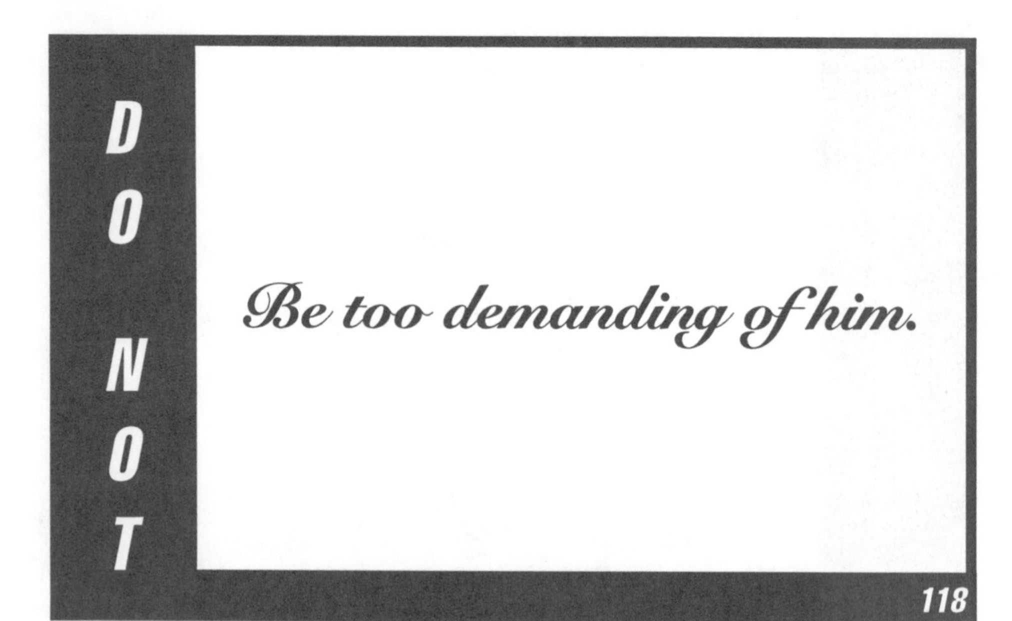
DO NOT
Be too demanding of him.
118

DO

Be playful sometimes.

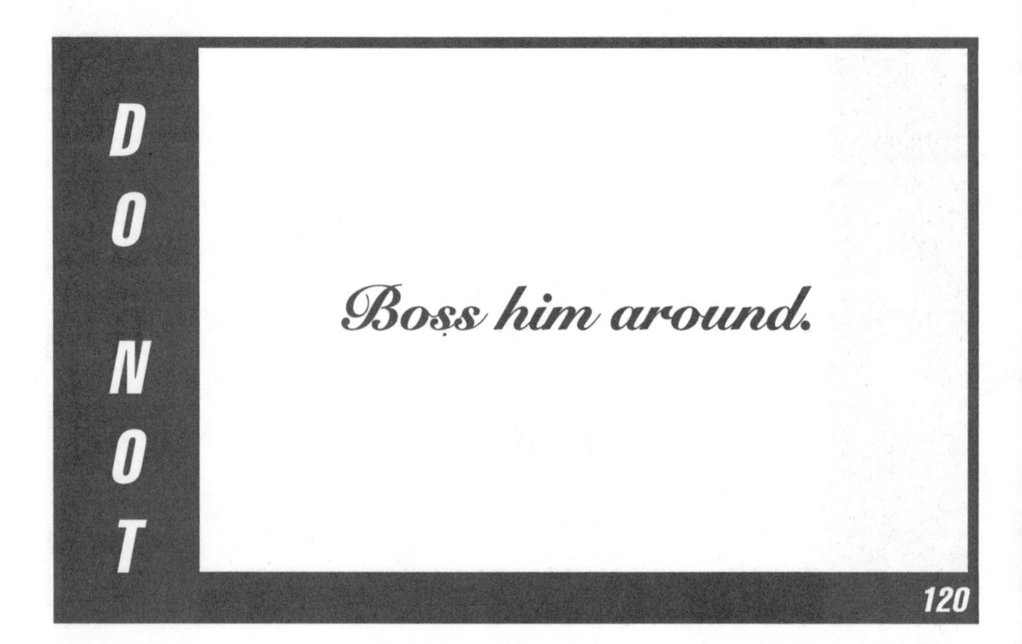
DO NOT
Boss him around.
120

DO

Tell him that he is your best friend.

DO NOT

Lack tact when expressing your dislikes and disappointments.

DO

Write poems to him.

DO NOT

Allow in-laws or friends to meddle in your relationship.

DO

Ask him about all of his favorites such as colors, sports, music, cologne, food, etc.

DO NOT

Be too proud to admit when you're wrong.

DO

Call him to see how his day is going.

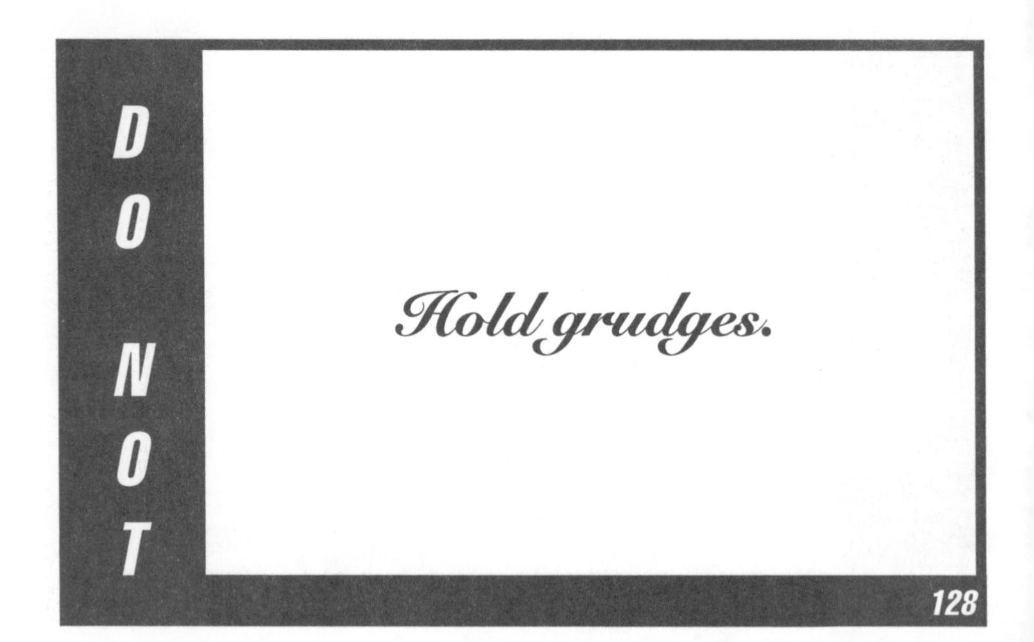
DO NOT
Hold grudges.
128

DO

Surprise him with cards and balloons.

D
O
N
O
T

Flirt with other men.

DO

Thank him for the things he does that make you feel loved.

DO NOT

Treat him as though his feelings do not count.

DO
Pray for him.

DO NOT

Compound his problems when he is already feeling disheartened and discouraged.

DO

Buy him tickets to sporting events to see his favorite teams and players.

DO NOT
Taunt him.
136

DO

Practice love through your actions.

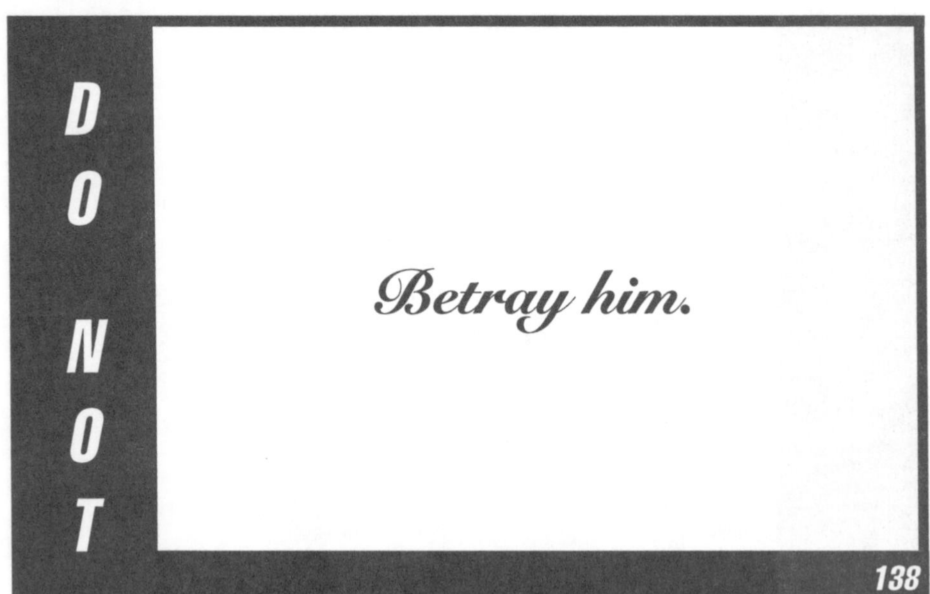
DO NOT
Betray him.
138

DO

Be decisive.

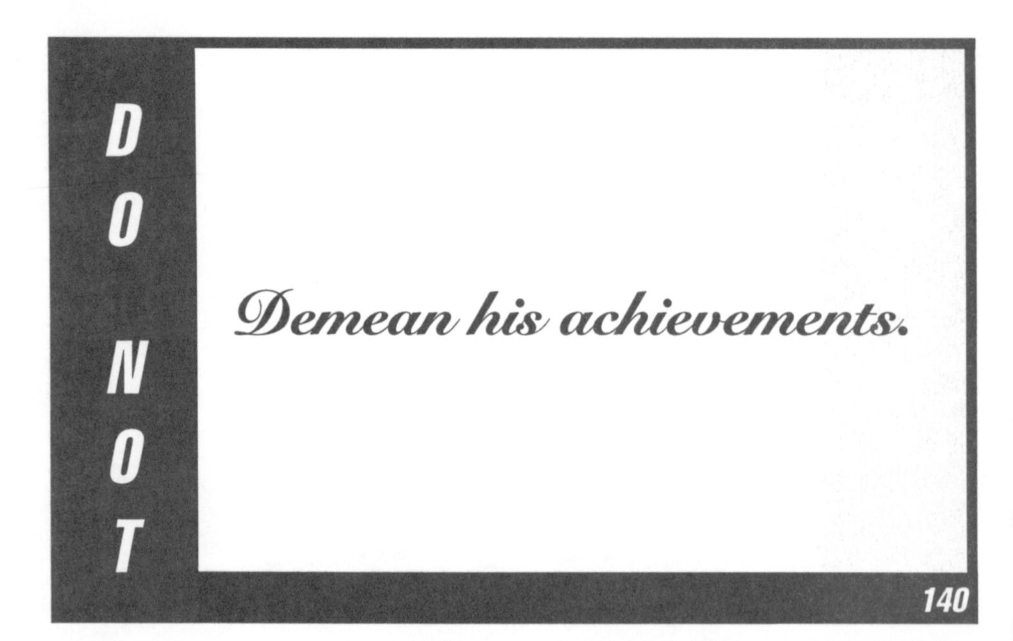
DO NOT
Demean his achievements.
140

DO

Buy him subscriptions to his favorite magazines.

DO NOT

Talk down to him in front of others or the children.

DO

Write him a letter occasionally, telling him how much you love him.

DO NOT

Take him for granted and make him feel unappreciated.

DO

Take the children for the day so that he can have time to be alone.

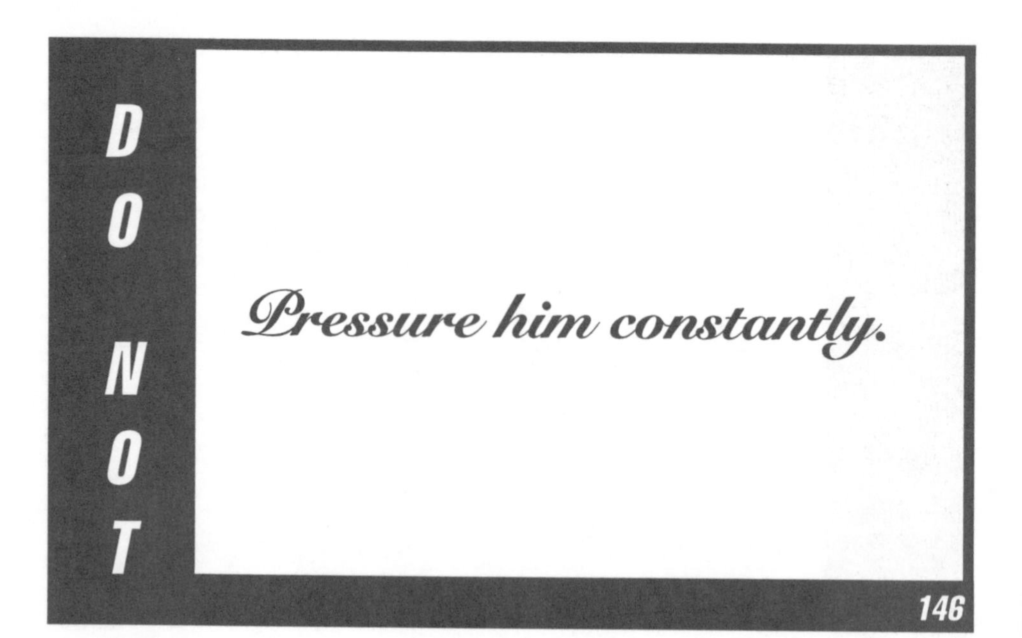
DO NOT
Pressure him constantly.
146

DO

Be expressive and affectionate.

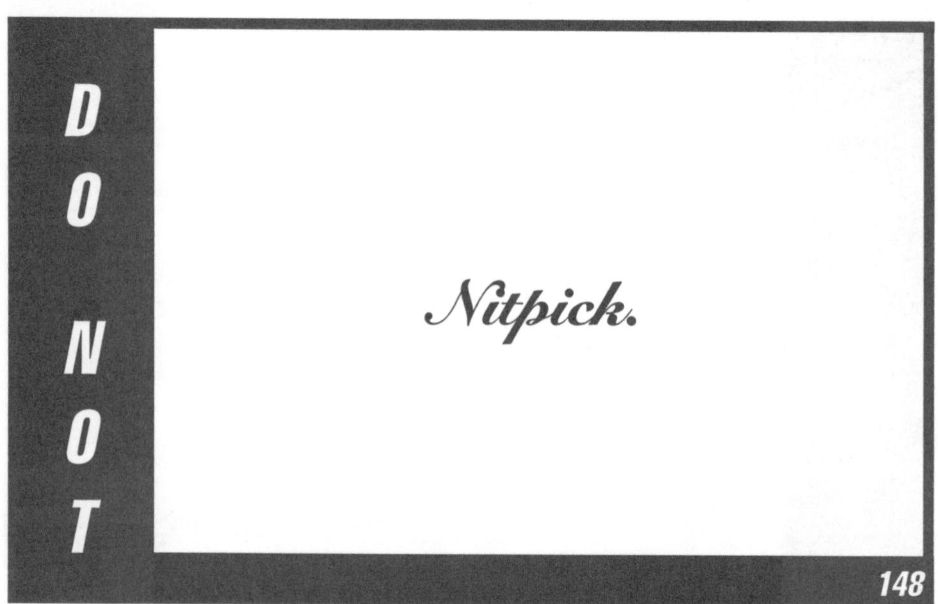
DO NOT
Nitpick.
148

DO

Do little things for him such as breakfast in bed, love notes in his wallet or briefcase, etc.

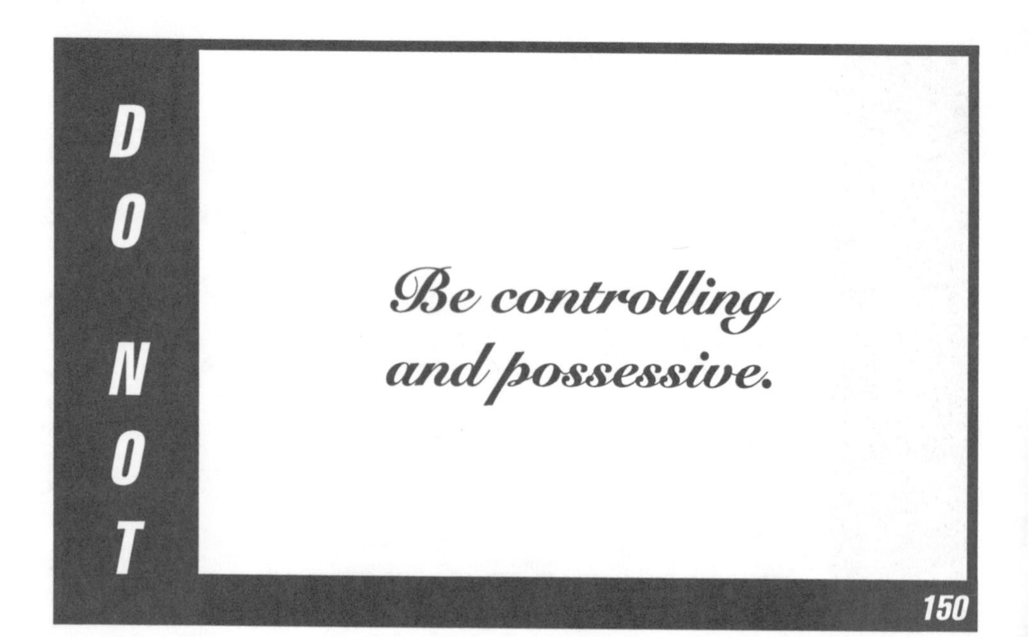
DO NOT
Be controlling
and possessive.
150

DO

Kiss him spontaneously.

DO NOT

Be spiteful.

DO

Smile when you see him.

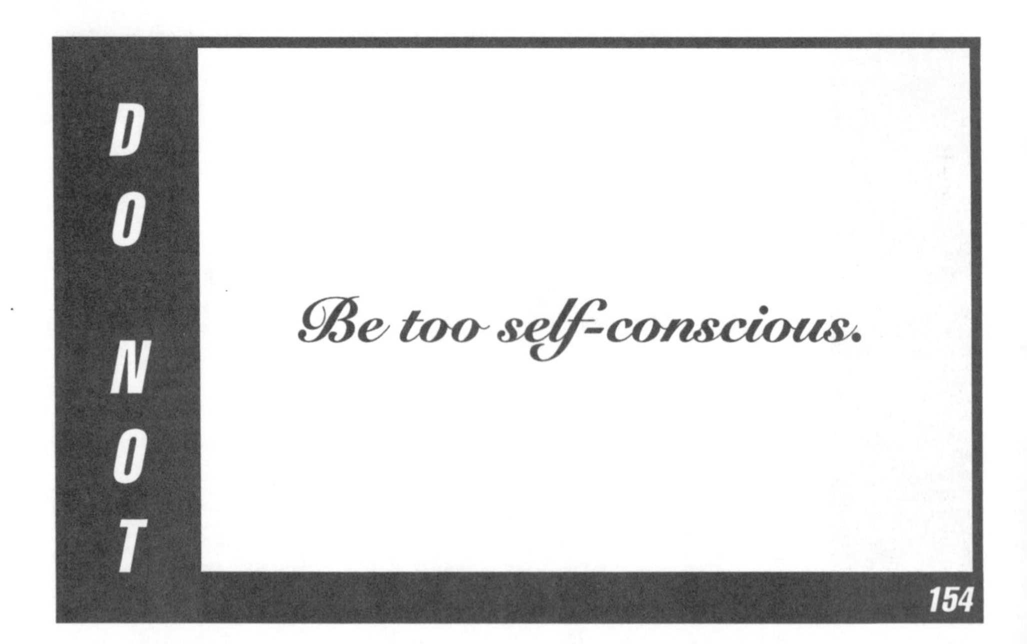
DO NOT
Be too self-conscious.

DO

Say what you mean and mean what you say.

DO NOT

Be a know-it-all.

DO

Create an intimate environment—candles, flowers, romantic music, etc.

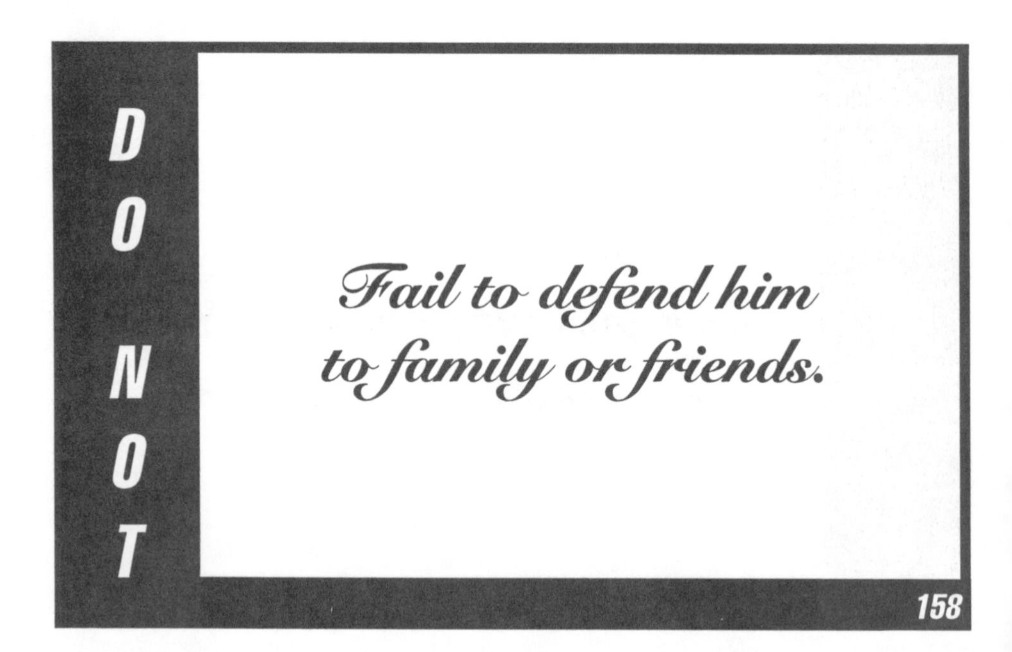
DO NOT
Fail to defend him
to family or friends.
158

DO

Keep abreast of current events and discuss them with him.

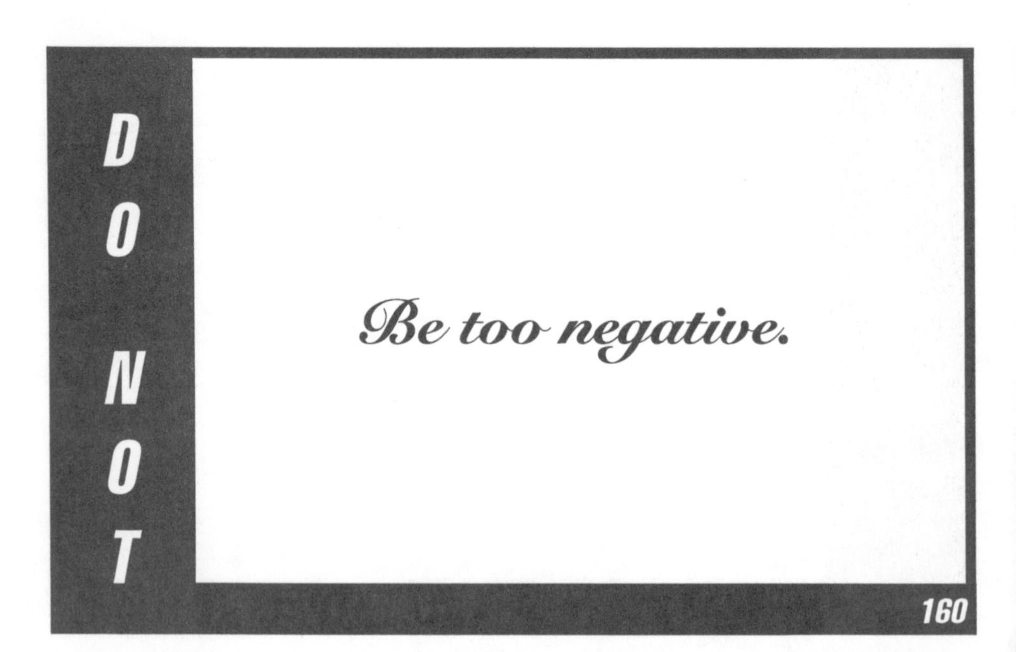
DO NOT
Be too negative.
160

DO

Find out your husband's favorite love song and then sing it to him.

DO NOT

Hold resentment
or being unforgiving.

DO

Surprise him.
Surprise him.
Surprise him.

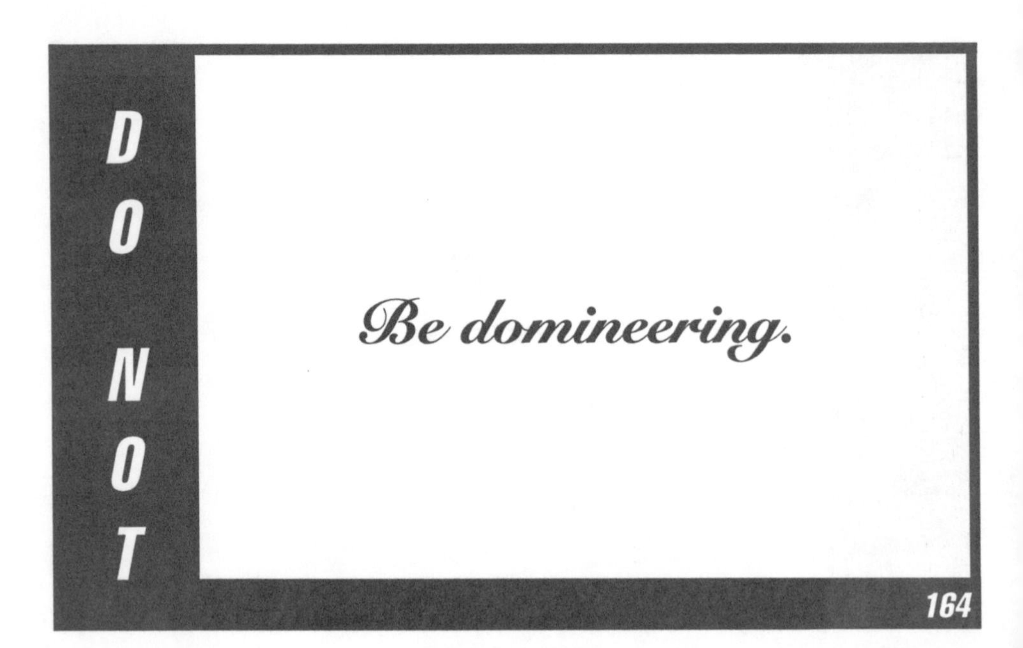
DO NOT
Be domineering.
164

DO

Be honest and sincere.

DO NOT

Fail to show an interest in his life and passions.

DO

Include your husband when making major decisions.

DO NOT

Fail to balance your personal, professional, and social lives.

DO

Try to weed out negativity and create a positive atmosphere.

DO NOT

Treat him like a girlfriend rather than a husband.

DO

Give him special coupons to be used in a day's notice. (i.e. favorite dinner, masquerade night, wish night, romance night, etc.) Be creative.

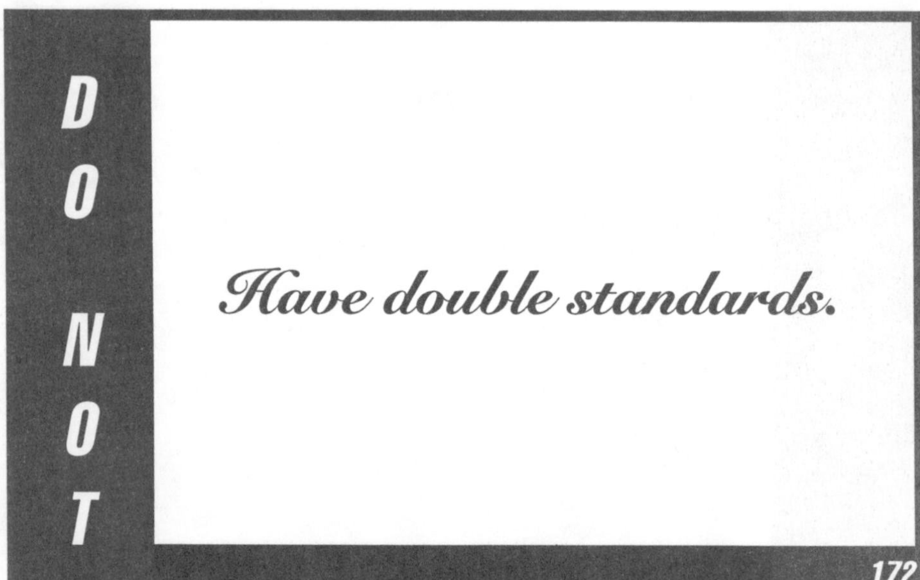
DO NOT
Have double standards.
172

DO

Ask him about his favorite stories, childhood memories, games, super heroes, mentors, etc., and share your own.

DO NOT

Be too moody or temperamental.

DO

Tell and show him that you admire and respect him.

DO NOT

Make him feel that if you had it to do over, you would marry someone else.

DO

Pamper your husband at times. Treat him to a day of grooming which includes a haircut, manicure, pedicure, and massage.

DO NOT

Fail to be supportive of his personal goals and aspirations.

DO

Escape to exotic places right at home. (i.e. Jamaican Night, with Jerk Chicken and reggae music; Hawaiian Luau Night with flower leis, and a hula dance.) Let your imagination soar.

DO NOT

Display an "I told you so" attitude when something goes wrong, rather than showing understanding and loving him through difficult times.

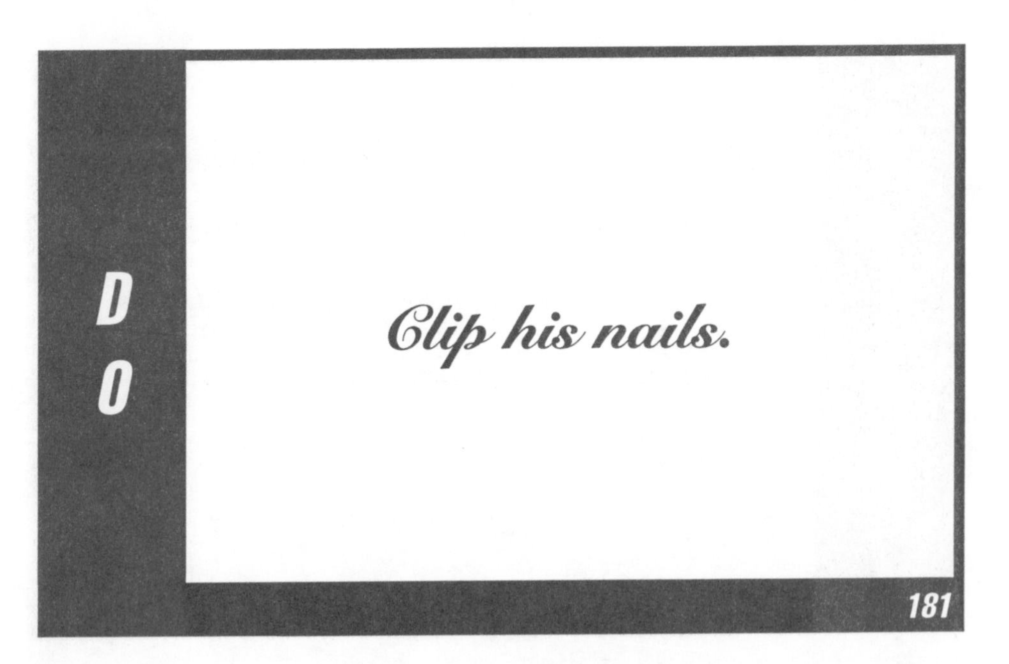
D
O
Clip his nails.
181

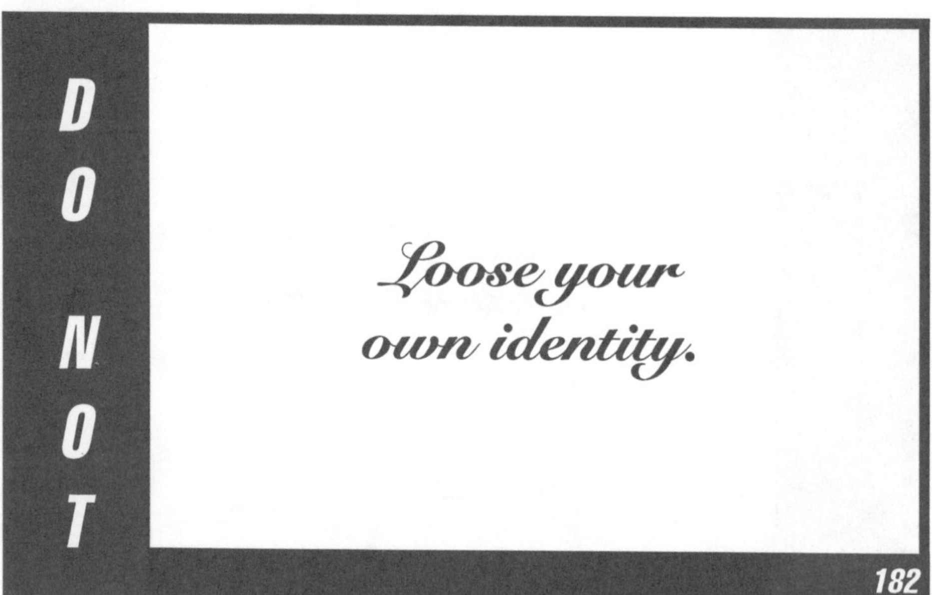
DO NOT
Loose your own identity.
182

DO

Always compliment him and tell him that you love him.

D
O
N
O
T

Blurt out his weaknesses in nonconstructive ways.

DO

Be willing to compromise—watch the programs and movies he prefers sometimes.

DO NOT

Abuse him verbally, emotionally, mentally, or physically.

DO

Flirt with your husband.

DO NOT

Be indecisive.

DO

Shampoo, condition, and brush his hair.

DO NOT

Let the sun go down on your wrath and go to bed angry.

DO

Be supportive of his goals.

DO NOT
Manipulate him.
192

DO

Help him to maintain his focus and accomplish his dreams.

DO NOT

Be more enthusiastic about other activities than about him.

DO

Remember that the way to a man's heart is through his stomach. Never underestimate the value of a great meal.

DO NOT

Be self-righteous.

D
O

Use variety to break up monotony.

DO NOT
Name-call.
198

DO

Treat your relationship like a living, breathing being. Always make certain that it is nurtured and growing, living and not dying.

D O N O T

Make a mountain out of a molehill.

DO

Remember that each and every annoyance or mistake is not grounds for battle.

DO NOT

Don't allow your children to manipulate you against your husband.

DO

Honor and respect him.

DO NOT

Lose self-control during arguments.

DO

Concentrate on the issue at hand during arguments–not the past.

D
O
N
O
T

Do not allow anyone to come between you two.

DO

Be sensitive in how you speak and use body language with your husband.

Husband 101

Everything Your Wife Wished You Already Knew

Husband 101 will give your marriage the "booster shot" you've been looking for. **Husband 101** will show you how to recapture the flame of your wife's passion for you again and again. **Husband 101** is a step-by-step mini-course in how to begin an engaging new love affair with your wife.

When you apply these simple ideas, your wife will connect with you at a much higher level. By taking every action in this book, you will automatically build a bridge to your wife's heart. She will begin to understand you dynamically because you will learn to speak the language of her heart-maybe for the first time. She will instantly begin to respond to you in exciting and meaningful new ways.

In **HUSBAND 101** you will:

- Discover the things that you wife may not openly tell you, but would love for you to do
- Take positive actions that will rejuvenate and revitalize your marriage
- Master your marriage by knowing how to unlock the precious treasures and hidden love your wife has been longing to share with you
- Capture the spark of burning passion in your relationship all over again . . . and discover ways to keep it fresh